W9-CZK-513

MERMAIDS

Cavendish
Square

New York

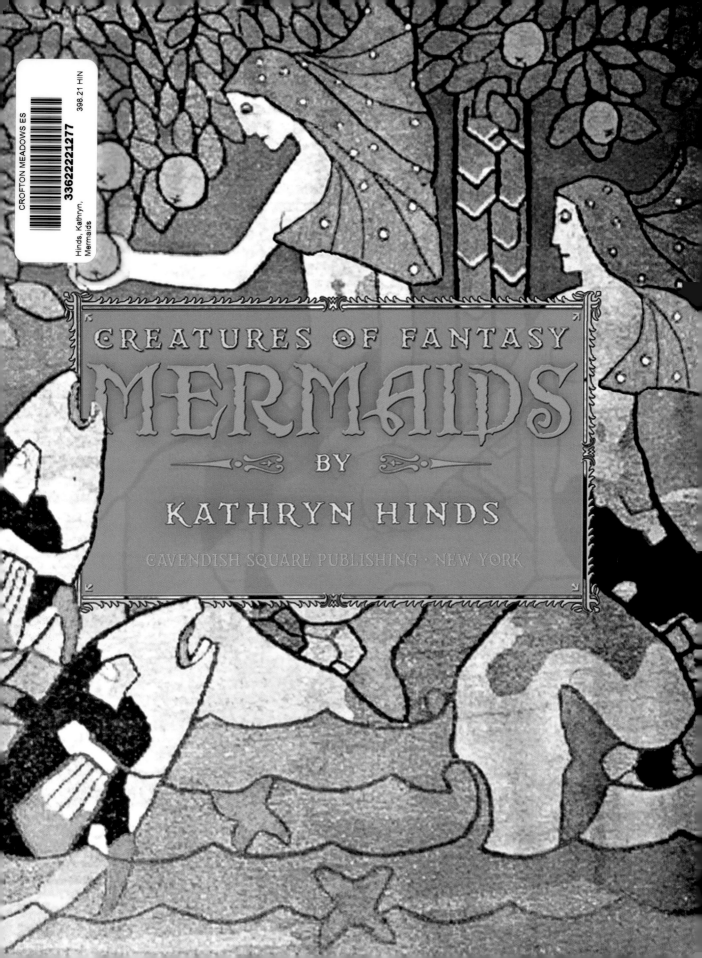

CREATURES OF FANTASY

MERMAIDS

BY

KATHRYN HINDS

CAVENDISH SQUARE PUBLISHING · NEW YORK

To Haven

Published in 2014 by Cavendish Square Publishing, LLC
303 Park Avenue South, Suite 1247, New York, NY 10010

LIBRARY OF CONGRESS CATALOGING-IN-PUBLICATION DATA
Hinds, Kathryn, 1962- Mermaids / Kathryn Hinds. p. cm.—(Creatures of fantasy) Summary: "Explores the mythical and historical backgrounds of mermaids including th Sirens, shape-shifters, Tritons, and the rusalka"—Provided by publisher. Includes bibliographical references (p.   ) and index. ISBN 978-0-7614-4924-9 (hardcover)—ISBN 978-1-62712-053-1 (paperback)— ISBN 978-1-60870-682-2 (ebook) 1. Mermaids—Juvenile literature. 2. Sirens (Mythology)—Juvenile literature. I. Title. GR910.H566 2013 398.21--dc23
2011045435

Editor: Joyce Stanton   Art Director: Anahid Hamparian   Series Designer: Michael Nelson

Photo research by Debbie Needleman. The photographs in this book are used by permission and through the courtesy of: Front Cover: © Illustrated London News Ltd/ Mary Evans Picture Library. Back Cover: © Laurie Lewis/Lebrecht Music & Arts. Pages i, 8: The Granger Collection, New York; pages ii-iii: Museum of Design & Decorative Arts, Copenhagen, Denmark. Photo by © Glenn Loney/ Everett Collection; page 6: Netsuke carved in the shape of a mermaid (ivory). Japanese School/Victoria & Albert Museum. London, UK/ The Bridgeman Art Library; page 11: © Erich Lessing/Art Resource, NY. Kunstmuseum, Basel, Switzerland; page 13: © V & A Images, London/Art Resource, NY. Victoria and Albert Museum, London, Great Britain; pages 14, 28, 35, 50: © Mary Evans Picture Library/ Alamy; pages 18, 20: © SuperStock; page 22: St. Brendan and a siren, from the German translation of "Navigatio Sancti Brendani Abbatis" c. 1476 (vellum), German School (15th century). Universitatsbibliothek, Heidelberg, Germany/The Bridgeman Art Library; page 25: Detail of gold mosaic floor, c. 1881. Leighton House Museum and Art Gallery, London, UK. Photo by Walter Crane/The Bridgeman Art Library/Getty Images; page 29: Married to a Mermaid, songsheet, 1860s/Private Collection/The Bridgeman Art Library; page 30: © Mary Evans Picture Library/ARTHUR RACKHAM/Everett Collection; pages 32, 33: © North Wind Picture Archives/Alamy; page 36: The Sea Bishop, illustration from "Omnium fere gentium nostraeque aetatis Nationum Habitus et Effigies" by Jean Sluperji, Antwerp, 1572 (color woodcut), Flemish School (16th century). Bibliotheque des Arts Decoratifs, Paris, France/Archives Charmet/The Bridgeman Art Library; page 39: The First Incarnation of Vishnu as Matsya "The Fish" The Deluge (paint on paper), Indian School. Victoria & Albert Museum, London, UK/Ann & Bury Peerless Picture Library/The Bridgeman Art Library; page 40: Monstrous Triton, Der Naturen Bloeme manuscript, KA_16_109v, c. 1350. National Library of the Netherlands; page 42: The Foresaken Merman, illustration from "Stories from the Poets" (color litho). Michael, Arthur C. (fl. 1903-28)/Private Collection/The Bridgeman Art Library; page 44: Water Sprites, 1899. Gustav Klimt/The Bridgeman Art Library/Getty Images; page 47: © Stock Montage/SuperStock; page 48: Kelpie Water Demon from "The World Guide to Gnomes, Fairies, Elves and Other Little People" by Thomas Keightley (1789-1872). Published 1880 (B&W engraving), American School (19th century)/Private Collection/The Stapleton Collection/The Bridgeman Art Library; page 57: © Image Asset Management Ltd/SuperStock.

Printed in the United States of America

front cover: Most mermaids have long hair, but this 1929 illustration depicts a mermaid with the fashionable short hair of the time.
back cover: A scene from an opera based on the legend of the rusalka, a mermaid-like Russian water spirit.
half-title: A mermaid princess from an 1890 collection of fairy tales.
title page: Mermaids frolic with young killer whales on a Danish wall hanging from around 1900.

CONTENTS

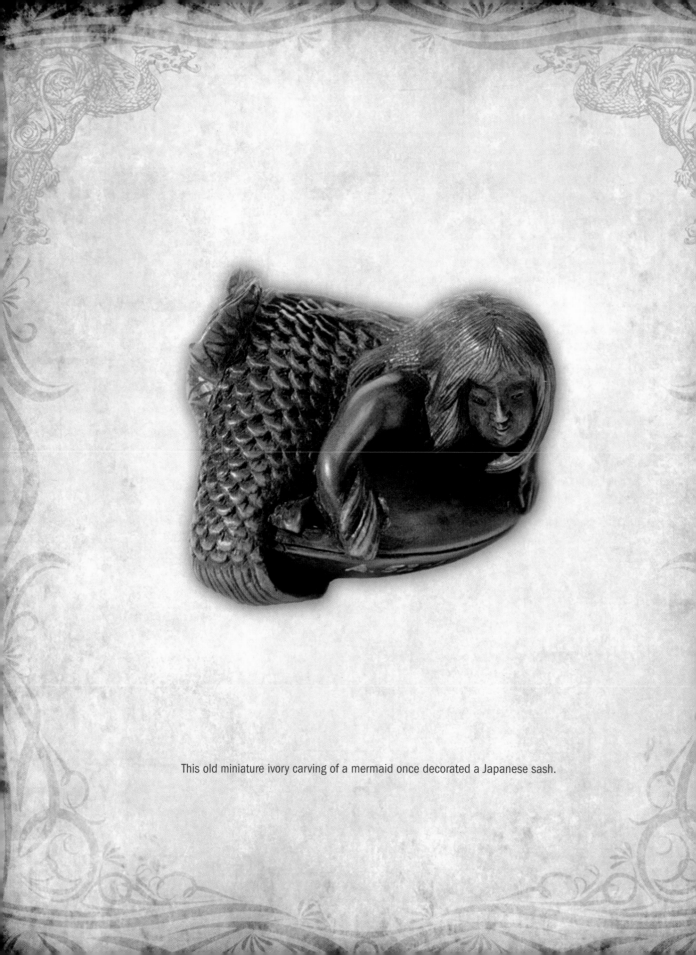

This old miniature ivory carving of a mermaid once decorated a Japanese sash.

INTRODUCTION

In the CREATURES OF FANTASY series, we celebrate the deeds of dragons, unicorns, mermaids, water monsters, and more. These fabulous beasts have inhabited the imagination and arts since the beginnings of human history. They have been immortalized in paintings and sculptures, mythology and literature, movies and video games. Today's blockbuster fantasy novels and films—*The Chronicles of Narnia, Harry Potter, Lord of the Rings, Eragon,* and others—have brought new popularity to the denizens of folklore, myths, and legends. It seems that these creatures of the imagination have always been with us and, in one way or another, always will be.

Belief in the fantastic, in wonders, appears to be a lasting part of the human experience. Even if we no longer believe that dragons and unicorns actually exist, we still like to think about what things might be like if they did. We dream and daydream about them. We make up stories. And as we share those dreams, read and tell those stories, we not only stir our imaginations but also explore some of the deepest hopes and fears of humanity. The power of the dragon, the purity of the unicorn, the wildness of the centaur, the allure of the mermaid—these and more are all part of our human heritage, the legends of our ancestors still alive for us today.

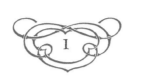

GODDESSES AND SPIRITS

[I] heard a mermaid on a dolphin's back
Uttering such dulcet and harmonious breath
That the rude sea grew civil at her song
And certain stars shot madly from their spheres
To hear the sea-maid's music.

~WILLIAM SHAKESPEARE, *A Midsummer Night's Dream*, 1590s

MERMAIDS. WHEN YOU HEAR THE WORD, the first thing you think of might be Ariel from the Disney film *The Little Mermaid*. Or maybe you remember the beautiful mermaids of Neverland in *Peter Pan*, who loved to bask on a rock in their lagoon, "combing out their hair in a lazy way. . . . The most haunting time at which to see them is at the turn of the moon, when they utter strange wailing cries; but the lagoon is dangerous for mortals then." Indeed, stories from around the world tell us that mermaids, no matter how lovely or lazy seeming, can pose a deadly threat to human beings. Or, sometimes, they can bring luck, love, happiness, and wealth to favored mortals. After all, these "sea maidens" are every bit as unpredictable and magnificent as the waters they live in.

Opposite: A 1932 illustration of the Little Mermaid, from a book of fairy tales by Hans Christian Andersen.

The First Mermaid

Thousands of years ago, people along the eastern coast of the Mediterranean Sea honored a goddess named Atargatis, also known as Derceto. She has been called a moon goddess, but clearly she was very concerned with fish, too. Her temples had sacred fishponds, and at one of them worshipers made offerings of fish crafted from gold and silver. Part fish herself, Derceto seems to have been the first being ever described as a mermaid.

A Roman writer who visited the eastern Mediterranean was shown a drawing of Derceto that portrayed her "in a curious form; for in the upper half she is woman, but from the waist to the lower extremities runs in the tail of a fish." An ancient Greek historian wrote that the goddess had only a woman's head, while the rest of her body was that of a fish—"and it is for this reason that the Syrians to this day abstain from this animal and honour their fish as gods." Despite this, it seems that many people in the region did eat seafood. In some cities, though, no one was allowed to catch fish without permission from the goddess, in the form of a fishing license sold by her priests.

Daughters of the Sea

The ancient Greeks and Romans believed that everything in nature had a kind of spirit. For them, water spirits were usually imagined as graceful, joyous young goddesses. The Greeks classified their sea goddesses in two groups. Those of the Mediterranean Sea were the Nereids, while those of the Atlantic Ocean were known as Oceanids. There were fifty Nereids, whose father was the god Nereus, the Old Man of the Sea. Their mother was Doris, an Oceanid, one of the three thousand daughters of Oceanus and

Nereids at play in a stormy sea, by Swiss artist Arnold Böcklin.

his wife Tethys, gigantic beings who were older than the great gods themselves.

One of the major Greek gods was Poseidon, lord of all the seas, and he married a Nereid, Amphitrite. Another famous Nereid was Thetis, who became the mother of the Greek warrior Achilles, renowned for his deeds during the Trojan War. After the Trojan War, Achilles's comrade Odysseus was delayed during his voyage back to Greece by an Oceanid named Calypso. Odysseus had angered Poseidon, so Poseidon caused a storm that wrecked his ship. Calypso rescued the weary warrior and kept him with her on her island. She wanted Odysseus to marry her and promised to make him immortal, but he longed to return to his wife and his own land. After seven years the gods took pity on Odysseus and convinced Calypso to help him build a ship and send him home.

The Greeks thought of their sea goddesses as wholly human. The Romans seem to have thought of the Nereids, at least sometimes, in the same way we imagine mermaids: part woman and part fish. And many believed there were Nereids who were actual sea creatures. The first-century Roman author and naval commander Pliny the Elder wrote about them in the section of his *Natural History* devoted to aquatic animals. He stated that the way Nereids were usually described was not "a fiction; only in them, the portion of the body that resembles the human figure is still rough all over with scales." Pliny knew this, he said, because a dying Nereid had been seen on the coast of Portugal, and even people far away from the beach had heard its sad song. He also recorded that, some decades earlier, "a considerable number of Nereids had been found dead upon the sea-shore" of what is now France.

In the Waters of India

Ancient scriptures from India tell of the Apsarases. Their name, it is said, means "moving in the water." There were several million of them, born from the churning of the ocean at the beginning of time. Although they belonged to the court of Indra, the god of the heavens, they were most often found around the sea and other bodies of water. Beautiful and playful, the Apsarases were also expert singers, dancers, and musicians. Sometimes a person might find an Apsaras's presence too distracting. If this happened, she could be sent away with a prayer like this one: "Where your gold and silver swings are, where cymbals and lutes chime together, thither do ye, O Apsaras, pass away."

The Hindu god Vishnu and his wife Lakshmi are carried on the cosmic ocean by Shesha, king of the Nagas.

Although Apsarases were usually joyful spirits, they did have a serious side. Not only could they could tell the future, but some warriors looked to them as guardians on the journey between life and death. These men knew that if they were killed on the battlefield, Apsarases would come to take them to Indra's celestial paradise.

Another kind of water spirit seems to have been partly related to dragons and partly to mermaids. India's Nagas could take the form of humans, multiheaded snakes, human-headed serpents, or humans with snake bodies or fish tails from the waist down. It was said there were a thousand of them, divided into four types. Hidden Nagas guarded treasure within the earth, and Heavenly Nagas protected the palaces of the gods. Divine Nagas created clouds and made the rain fall. Earthly Nagas kept rivers and water outlets clear, although they could drain these water sources if they were angered. The Earthly Nagas lived in lakes and rivers as well as the ocean. Their most glorious palaces, bedecked with emeralds, rubies, and gold, lay at the bottom of the sea.

SINGING SIRENS

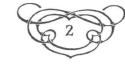

Featherless birds, legless maidens, finless fish—what can they be?
~ANDREAS ALCIATUS, *Emblemata*, 1531

A S YOU LEARN MORE ABOUT MERMAIDS, you may sometimes see them referred to as Sirens. This is a very old name, which goes back to ancient Greece and Rome. The Sirens of Greco-Roman myth and legend were fantastic creatures that were part woman and were associated with the dangers of the sea. They were first written about in the *Odyssey*, the famous epic by the Greek poet Homer. This long, exciting poem told the story of the hero Odysseus's adventures on his ten-year journey home after the Trojan War.

Homer never described what the Sirens looked like, but ancient Greek vase paintings show them as birds with the heads of women. That was probably how most Greeks and Romans thought of them. For example, a fourth-century Roman poet named Claudianus

Opposite:
In Greek and Roman mythology, the only mortal who sang more enchantingly than the Sirens was Orpheus, whose music saved his shipmates when they sailed past the Sirens' island.

called the Sirens "bird-maidens . . . [whose] music, gentle danger of the sea, was pleasurable terror among the waves."

During the first century, however, the Roman poet Ovid had referred to the Sirens as *monstra maris*, "monsters of the sea." Ovid's books were very popular in later centuries, and his writings may have given people the idea that Sirens had a fishlike quality. In any case, by the tenth century some European authors had begun describing the Sirens as part women and part fish. Other writers thought there were different types of Sirens, including fish-women, bird-women, and snake-women. By 1300 there was general agreement that Sirens were what we think of as mermaids.

Another thing most writers had agreed on was that Sirens symbolized the dangers of temptation. Around 1210 a French author, Guillaume Le Clerc, summed it up:

> The siren, who sings so sweetly
> And enchants folk by her song
> Affords example for instructing those
> Who through this world must voyage.
> We who through the world do pass
> Are deceived by such a sound,
> By the glamour, by the [desires]
> Of this world, which kill us
> When we have tasted such pleasures.

TEMPTED HEROES

The ancient Greek hero Odysseus certainly experienced the temptation of the Sirens. At one point in his adventures, he spent some time on the island of the witch-goddess Circe. As he prepared to

sail away, she warned him that he would soon encounter the Sirens, "who bewitch everybody that approaches them. There is no homecoming for the man who draws near them unaware and hears the Sirens' voices. . . . For with the music of their song, the Sirens cast their spell upon him, as they sit there in a meadow piled high with the mouldering skeletons of men."

To get safely past the Sirens, Circe told Odysseus, he must plug his men's ears with beeswax. She knew that he himself would be overcome by curiosity to hear the Sirens' music, so she also advised him to have his men tie him tightly to the ship's mast. That way, no matter how much the song filled him with longing to join the Sirens, he would not be able to jump overboard.

Circe was right. As Odysseus's ship approached the Sirens' island, they sang, "Come hither, come, Odysseus. . . . Bring in your ship, and listen to our song. For none has ever passed us in a black-hulled ship till from our lips he heard ecstatic song, then went his way rejoicing and with larger knowledge." It was a good thing Odysseus had taken Circe's advice, because, as he told a friend later, "So spoke they, sending forth their glorious song, and my heart longed to listen. Knitting my brows, I signed my men to set me free; but bending forward, on they rowed."

In this way Odysseus and his men passed the Sirens in safety. Only once before had a ship successfully escaped their temptation. The Greek hero Jason had sailed his vessel, the *Argo*, to a land on the eastern shore of the Black Sea to obtain a magical object, the Golden Fleece.* He was successful in his quest, but on his journey home he was forced to sail near the island of the Sirens. Luckily, he had a whole crew of heroes on board the *Argo*. One of them was the great singer and musician Orpheus. When the Sirens began to

*More of this story is told in another book in this series, *Dragons.*

English artist John William Waterhouse's 1891 painting of Odysseus and the Sirens shows the tempting singers in their most ancient form, part woman and part bird.

sing, Orpheus did, too. His song was so beautiful and inspired that the crew listened to him instead of to the Sirens. In fact, according to the first-century Roman writer Seneca:

> The sound of Orpheus the Thracian's lyre
> Almost forced the Sirens who beckon ships
> To follow that sound.

The Sirens managed to resist the lure of Orpheus's song, but a school of music-loving dolphins swam after the *Argo* for as long as he continued to play.

IRRESISTIBLE MUSIC

Why was the Sirens' song so powerful? Some writers have thought the magic was in the music itself—the unearthly melodies and heavenly harmonies, which made all human music sound like meaningless noise. And surely no mortal woman's voice could be as beautiful and haunting as the voices of the Sirens.

Others have believed it was not so much the music as the words that had such a powerful effect. The song the Sirens sang to Odysseus ended, "We know all things that come to pass on the bounteous

Earth." This line inspired the Roman writer Cicero to say, "It was not the sweetness of their voices or the novelty and diversity of their songs, but their professions of knowledge which used to attract the passing voyagers. . . . It is *knowledge* that the Sirens offer."

Perhaps, though, the Sirens sang different songs to different voyagers; perhaps each person who heard them heard a song about his or her own heart's desires. Not everyone longed for knowledge the way Odysseus and Cicero did. Most authors have thought the Sirens sang about more down-to-earth delights. The nineteenth-century artist and writer William Morris imagined that the Sirens' song tempted sailors with promises of an enchanted life:

> Come to the land where none grows old,
> And none is rash or over-bold,
> Nor any noise there is of war,
> Or rumour from wild lands afar,
> Or plagues, or birth and death of kings. . . .
> Alone with us, dwell happily,
> Beneath our trembling roof of sea.

Wasn't freedom from hardship, disease, and conflict what anyone would yearn for? The Sirens' singing made these desires even more intense, and their lovely faces and voices reinforced the appeal of the life they described. The problem was, it was an impossible life: only in death could people truly be free of all sorrows. Perhaps this was what the Sirens were really singing about—after all, no living person could dwell beneath their "trembling roof of sea." In any case, whatever the song really meant, it was so beautiful that, as Claudianus wrote, a sailor hearing it "longed not to take the secure route home."

From her high rock, the Lorelei watches for boatmen on the Rhine River.

The Lorelei

German folklore had its own version of the Sirens who lured sailors to their death. This northern water spirit, the Lorelei, lived at a narrow point of the Rhine River where there were large, high rocks and dangerous currents. A famous poem by nineteenth-century German writer Heinrich Heine tells the story of one boatman's tragic encounter with the Lorelei. Here is an English translation of the poem's ending:

> High yonder in wondrous seeming,
> Reclines a maiden fair,
> Her golden jewels are gleaming
> And she combs her golden hair.
>
> A comb of gold is she plying
> And warbles a wondrous song,
> That a thrilling melody sighing,
> Floats like a spell along.
>
> The boatman his bark while steering,
> Is seized in a wild amaze;
> He heeds not the rocks that are nearing,
> Fixed high is his spell-bound gaze.
>
> And soon by the waters swallowed,
> Will bark and boatman lie;
> Such fatal charm weaves ever
> The song of the Lorelei.

FISH-TAILED MAIDENS

Then up . . . raised the mermaiden,
Wi' the comb an' glass in her hand:
"Here's a health to you, my merry young men,
For you never will see dry land."
~"SIR PATRICK SPENS," SCOTTISH BALLAD, 1700S

DURING THE MIDDLE AGES (ABOUT 500-1500) in Europe, many real creatures were little understood and seemed fantastical, such as giraffes and hippopotamuses. Many fantastical creatures, on the other hand, seemed entirely real, including mermaids. Books by respected authorities described them, and there were countless stories and ballads about them. They even appeared in carvings on the stone walls and wooden seats of churches. Moreover, there were plenty of reports of mermaid sightings, and not just from fishermen and sailors but also from educated churchmen.

Opposite: "The Voyage of Saint Brendan," a popular tale during the Middle Ages, tells of the early Irish saint's encounters with mermaids, sea monsters, magical islands, and other wonders during his seven years of sailing the ocean.

Saints and Sea Folk

According to a book written by an Englishman in about 1211, the waters around the British Isles were full of mermaids and mermen. Whether or not this was true, these islands were certainly home to many mermaid stories. Several early tales concern encounters between merpeople and Christian holy men. For example, Irish legends tell how Saint Patrick converted an ancient merman named Fintan to Christianity. When, however, a group of women ignored Patrick's preaching and insisted on keeping their old religion, he turned them into mermaids and cast them into the sea.

A saint on the island of Iona, off the west coast of Scotland, was visited every day by a beautiful mermaid. Over and over she begged the holy man to give her a soul. His response was always the same: if she wanted a soul, she must leave the sea and never return to it. Every time the mermaid heard this, she sobbed and pleaded with the saint, but neither her tears nor her beauty moved him. The mermaid was in despair because not only did she long for a soul, but she had fallen in love with the saint. Nothing, however, was stronger than her love for the sea, and she could not bear to leave it. She paid the saint one final visit, he denied her a soul one final time, and then she disappeared into the ocean depths forever.

There was a famous Irish mermaid named Liban, who started out as a normal young woman. Near her home was a sacred well, but people neglected it and it overflowed, creating a large lake now known as Lough Neagh. For a year Liban miraculously remained alive, along with her favorite dog, in a room on the bottom of the lake. But she grew tired of being trapped there, and prayed to be turned into a salmon so that she could swim around freely in the water. Her prayer was half answered: her legs became a salmon's tail, while the rest of

her remained a woman. Now Liban was able to swim not only in her lake but in the ocean as well. Her dog had been transformed into an otter, which swam beside her "wherever she went as long as she lived in the sea."

Liban remained this way for three hundred years. Then one day in the year 558, she was caught in a fishing net. The fisherman took her to shore and kept her in a boat partly filled with water so that people could come and marvel at her. After a while, though, two saints took her to a church. They told her she could live on the land for as long as she'd lived in the water, or she could choose to die and go to heaven right after they baptized her. Liban decided she didn't want to spend three hundred years on land, so she accepted baptism and then simply died. More than a thousand years later, in the 1700s, people continued to say that there were mermaids in Lough Neagh. And whoever ventured past the lake did so cautiously, "expecting every moment to be captured and carried off by the witching mere-maidens."

A musical mermaid and her fish companion, created by fairy-tale illustrator Walter Crane to decorate the wall of a fellow artist's London home around 1880.

DANGEROUS DAMSELS

To many people in the Middle Ages, mermaids were a danger to both body and soul. As we saw with Guillaume Le Clerc's description of the Siren, writers often used mermaids as symbols of the things that could tempt Christians away from the path to heaven. Guillaume listed some of these evils, including "bodily ease," overeating, drunkenness, laziness, riches, "fat horses," and fancy or expensive clothing.

So great is our delight in them
That perforce we fall asleep.
Thereupon the siren kills us.

Mermaids posed another kind of danger because, it was believed, they didn't have souls. Yet many deeply desired a soul, and the easiest way to obtain one was to take it from a living person. This was one of the reasons mermaids carried off and drowned people. Another reason was loneliness—or hunger. According to a writer in the early 1200s, "This wonderful beast is glad and merry in tempest, and sad and heavy in fair weather. With sweetness of song this beast maketh shipmen to sleep, and when she seeth that they are asleep, she goeth into the ship." She would seize a sailor and take him away, and if he did not fall in love with her, she killed and ate him.

Another problem with mermaids was that they had bad tempers. There were numerous stories of sailors or fishermen who somehow offended a mermaid. She would then take revenge by creating a sandbar to choke the local harbor, by making the fish disappear, by causing a flood, or by drowning the offender. Sailors also feared mermaids because they were unpredictable and could stir up fierce storms just on a whim. If seamen spotted a mermaid following or staring at their ship, they could be pretty sure a bad storm was coming, one that none of them was likely to survive.

Although mermaids were a threat at sea, on land they were sometimes tameable. In 1403 a mermaid was washed ashore in a flood in the Netherlands. After the waters receded, she was stranded in the low-lying fields. Some women going out to milk their cows spotted her and decided to take her home with them. But, says a book from

1635, "first they cleansed her of the sea-moss, which did stick about her." The women clothed the mermaid, fed her bread and milk, and taught her to spin and to kneel before the cross. She was apparently treated as a servant, since we are told "she would obey her mistress." Her new life did not seem to make her happy: she "would often strive to steal again into the sea, but being carefully watched, she could not. . . . She never spoke, but lived dumb and continued alive (as some say) fifteen years; then she died."

MARRIED TO A MERMAID

For nearly as long as people have been telling stories about mermaids, there have been tales of men who married them. Sometimes a mermaid took her human husband to live in her palace or cave under the sea—dwellings fabled for their splendor, decorated with coral, pearls, and treasures from the holds of sunken ships. Sometimes the mermaid went to live on land with her husband, but there were always conditions to such marriages, and they often ended unhappily.

Perhaps the most famous mermaid wife was Melusine, whose story was known throughout Europe. In 1387 a French writer collected all the versions of the tale he could find, producing a book hundreds of pages long. The basic story goes like this:

One day a young French nobleman named Raymond was out hunting in the forest, where he came across a fountain. Sitting beside it was a perfectly normal-looking but very beautiful young woman, Melusine. Raymond immediately fell in love with her, and she returned his feelings. Soon they were married. Melusine provided their home, a magnificent castle. But she would continue to live there with Raymond only on one condition: every Saturday he

Melusine, her true nature discovered, bids farewell forever to her untrusting husband.

must leave her alone in her room. If he dared to enter or even peek in, their marriage would be over.

Everything went well for a long time, except that all Melusine and Raymond's children were born with some kind of deformity. Eventually people began to gossip about Melusine and to wonder what it was she did every Saturday. Their talk made Raymond suspicious about his wife's desire for privacy. When he couldn't stand it any longer, he cautiously peered through the keyhole of her room. He saw her taking a bath—and her legs had turned into a fish tail!

When Melusine discovered that Raymond had broken his promise, she disappeared through the castle window. He never saw her again. Some versions of the story say she turned into a dragon and flew away. It was also said that for some time she returned to the castle every night to nurse her two youngest sons. Not only did she continue to look after her children, but she watched over all their descendants, too. Many noble families of Europe were proud to trace their ancestry to Melusine.

The Lady of Lake Fan Fach

In the folklore of Wales, in western Great Britain, there are female fairies who live in streams and lakes. Although they may not have fish tails, they behave much like mermaids. The best known of these Welsh water spirits is the Lady of Lake Fan Fach.

Near the end of the twelfth century, a young man herding sheep and goats beside this lake saw a beautiful woman "sitting on the unruffled surface of the water. . . . Her hair flowed gracefully in ringlets over her shoulders, the tresses of which she arranged with a comb, whilst the glassy surface of her watery couch served for the purpose of a mirror." The young man fell in love with her, and in time she agreed to marry him. She warned him, though, that if he struck her three times without good reason, she would leave him forever.

The lady brought many cows, horses, sheep, and goats with her to the marriage, and the couple prospered. They remained very much in love, yet on two occasions the husband struck his wife—only light taps, really, but that was enough; one more blow, and he would never see his wife again. They had three fine, clever sons, and they were happy for many more years.

Then one day they went to a funeral, and the lady laughed, rejoicing "because people when they die go out of trouble." Her husband was so shocked at her behavior "that he touched her, saying, 'Hush! hush! don't laugh.'" This disapproving touch was enough to end the marriage. She immediately rose up, called all her livestock to her, and disappeared with them into the Lake of Fan Fach.

What happened to her husband afterward is unknown. The three sons, however, often wandered by the lakeside, hoping their mother might reappear and speak with them. Eventually she did, and she showed them healing herbs and taught them various ways to treat diseases and injuries. They became renowned physicians, who not only served great nobles but also gave free medical care to the poor, as did their sons, grandsons, and great-grandsons after them.

STRANGE SIGHTINGS

The mermaids and men-fish seem to me
the most strange fish in the waters.
~John Swan, *Speculum Mundi*, 1635

W RITINGS ABOUT MERMAIDS FROM THE Middle Ages often tended to be like fairy tales or to be a way of teaching moral lessons. This started to change as Europeans threw themselves into the exploration and colonization of other parts of the world. More ships out on the waters, voyaging to new and distant places, meant there were more mermaid sightings.

At the same time, some people began to doubt the existence of mermaids. Others, however, were eager to understand more about their place in nature and to study them in a scientific manner. For example, in 1560 fishermen in Sri Lanka, a large island south of India, caught seven merpeople in their nets. A doctor from the Portuguese colony in India dissected the corpses and pronounced

Opposite: A 1901 illustration by Arthur Rackham shows the classic mermaid of legend and story, singing as she combs her long hair.

English explorer Henry Hudson, one of many seamen who reported sightings of mermaids.

the creatures to be very humanlike. (Most other people who got close to mermaids were content just to observe them.)

SAILORS' TALES

As a sample of the many seafarers' descriptions of mermaids, let's look at the reports of three experienced, knowledgeable English captains. In 1608 Henry Hudson was exploring the Arctic Ocean. In the ship's log he recorded that two of his men saw a mermaid on June 15. He wrote, "From the navel upward, her back and breasts were like a woman's. . . . Her skin was very white; and long hair hanging down behind, of color black; in her going down they saw her tail, which was like the tail of a porpoise, and speckled like a mackerel."

Two years later, Richard Whitbourne described at length a creature he saw in Newfoundland, Canada. In a harbor he spotted something swimming toward him; judging by its face and neck, it looked like a woman:

> It seemed to be so beautiful, and in those parts so well proportioned, having round about upon the head all blue streaks, resembling hair, down to the neck . . . and seeing the same coming so swiftly towards me, I stepped back. . . . Which when this strange creature saw that I went from it, it presently thereupon dived a little under water, . . . whereby I beheld the shoulders and back down to the middle, to be as square, white and smooth as the back of a man, and from the middle to the hinder part, pointing in proportion like a broad hooked arrow.

Whitbourne concluded his account, "This (I suppose) was a mermaid." But whether what he'd seen was *really* a mermaid, he wrote, "I know not; I leave it for others to judge."

Captain John Smith had his doubts, too, when he spotted something off the coast of a Caribbean island in 1614. At first he thought it was a woman, "swimming with all possible grace near the shore. . . . [It had] large eyes, rather too round, a finely shaped nose (a little too short), well-formed ears, rather too long, and her long green hair imparted to her an original character by no means unattractive." Smith thought he might be falling in love with her—until she moved in a way that revealed that "from below the waist the woman gave way to the fish," and he knew she was in fact a mermaid.

A 1598 map of the Arctic coast of Russia, the region where two of Hudson's men thought they saw a mermaid.

Mermaidology

In his 1635 book *Speculum Mundi*, or *Mirror of the World*, English author John Swan tried to describe the world and the place of things in God's creation. He was in no doubt that mermaids were part of the creation—but he did question some of the common opinions about them. "Some have supposed them to be devils or spirits, in regard of their whooping noise they make. For (as if they had power to raise extraordinary storms and tempests), the winds blow, seas rage, and clouds drop . . . after they seem to call."

Swan did not believe mermaids caused storms. It was more reasonable to think that mermaids, like many other creatures, could naturally sense weather changes before those changes were obvious to humans. Perhaps, then, the mermaids' cries were just a reaction to bad weather moving in. But what about storms that arose with extreme suddenness? Swan theorized that such storms were raised "by the thickening and breaking of the air; which the snortling rushing and howling of these beasts, assembled in an innumerable company, causeth. For it is certain that sounds will break and alter the air." In any case, mermaids might have some hidden powers "to work strange feats, and yet be neither spirits nor devils: for experience likewise teacheth, that they die either sooner or later after their taking."

An example of the short life span of a captured mermaid occurred in the early 1700s, when one was caught off the coast of Borneo in Southeast Asia. Close to five feet long, it was slender like an eel. According to the caption of a picture of it in a book by a Dutch naturalist, "It lived on land for four days, and seven hours in a barrel filled with water. From time to time it uttered little cries like that of a mouse. Although offered small fish, molluscs, crabs, crayfish, etc., it would not eat."

The eighteenth-century Norwegian bishop and naturalist Erik Pontoppidan believed firmly in the existence of mermaids. He wrote that in Bergen, Norway, "There are several hundreds of persons of credit and reputation who affirm, with the strongest assurance, that they have seen this kind of creature." Even one of the greatest scientists of the 1700s, Swedish naturalist Carl Linnaeus—the man who invented our system of scientific names for plants and animals— thought the existence of mermaids might be possible. But it was equally possible, he said, that they were simply "fable and fantasy."

MERMAIDS OR MANATEES?

On January 9, 1493, Christopher Columbus was sailing along the northern coast of Haiti when he had a startling experience: "I saw three sirens, that came up very high out of the sea. They are not as beautiful as they are painted, since in some ways they have a face like a man." He called them "sirens" because mermaids were what he expected to see—and yet these were not exactly what he'd expected mermaids to look like. They were in fact manatees, aquatic mammals that inhabit the tropical waters of the eastern Americas and West Africa.

A great many mermaid sightings can probably be explained by the manatee and its two cousins, the dugong of the Indian Ocean and western Pacific, and Steller's sea cow, which is now extinct but used to live in the Bering Sea between Russia and Alaska. Although these mammals do not resemble beautiful maidens at all, they can seem humanlike in many ways—especially when seen from a distance, possibly in foggy or twilit waters, by sailors who have been away from land for a long time. Because of all the cases of mistaken identity, the scientific classification these mammals belong to has been named Sirenia.

Seals and other animals might also have been mistaken for merpeople. For example, a twelfth-century book from Iceland told about a creature spotted near Greenland that looked exactly like a human from the waist up, while the rest resembled a fish. "The hands seem to people to be long, and the fingers not to be parted, but united by a web like that on the feet of water-birds. . . . [It had] a very horrible face, with broad brow and piercing eyes, a wide mouth and double chin." At the time the creature was thought to be some kind of merperson. The description, however—especially of its face—makes it sound very much like a walrus.

MERMEN

Amongst sea-monsters which are in the North Sea,
and are often seen, I shall give the first place
to the Hav-manden, or merman.

~ERIK PONTOPPIDAN, *Natural History of Norway*, 1755

A CCORDING TO MANY OLD STORIES, ONE OF the reasons mermaids often wanted human husbands was because mermen were extremely ugly. Some people believed that when a mermaid married a merman, she became just as ugly as he was. Not all mermen were hideous to look at, though. Some were appealing enough to win human brides. Some were even divine.

MERGODS

One of the world's earliest known deities was a merman. Worshiped in the Middle East starting more than six thousand years ago, his name was Ea. He was portrayed as a dignified bearded man with a

Opposite: A bishop fish. When one was caught in Poland in 1531, priests returned it to the water after seeing it make the sign of the cross.

fish tail instead of legs, or as a man wrapped in a fish-shaped cloak, its hood formed by the fish's head. As we might expect, Ea was a god of the sea, of fish, and of shipping—but he was also a god of civilization, as an ancient Greek historian tells us:

> This Being in the daytime used to converse with men . . . and he gave them an insight into letters and sciences, and every kind of art. He taught them to construct houses, to found temples, to compile laws, and explained to them the principles of geometrical knowledge. He made them distinguish the seeds of the earth, and showed them how to collect fruits. . . . When the sun set, it was the custom of this Being to plunge again into the sea and abide all night in the deep.

The Indian god Vishnu also had a merman form. As the preserver of creation, working constantly for the good of the world, Vishnu appeared on the earth during times of great emergency. On each occasion, he took a different shape. When a demon stole the sacred scriptures and caused a world-destroying flood, Vishnu became Matsya, the Fish, and helped a wise king rescue all the earth's plants and animals. As soon as they were safe, Matsya dove beneath the floodwaters, defeated the demon, and retrieved the scriptures. Once the holy writings were returned to their rightful place, the world was restored. Statues and paintings of Matsya show him as a typical merman or as a man emerging from the head and body of a fish. He has four arms, holding various weapons and often a conch shell.

According to the ancient Greeks, the conch-shell trumpet was invented by Triton, the fish-tailed son of Poseidon and Amphitrite.

The defeated demon lying before him and the holy scriptures safe in his hands, Vishnu—as Matsya, the Fish—rescues the surviving humans from the floodwaters.

When Triton blew on his trumpet, he could frighten the enemies of the gods or, with a different note, calm the waves. Ovid told how, after a great flood had drowned the land, Triton rose from the bottom of the sea, "his shoulders barnacled with sea-shells. . . . He raised his horn . . . that, sounded in mid ocean, fills the shores of dawn and sunset round the world; and when it touched the god's wet-bearded lips and took his breath and sounded the retreat, all the wide waters of the land and sea heard it, and all, hearing its voice, obeyed."

Triton gave his name to the Tritons, mermen who lived in the Mediterranean Sea and were the male counterparts of the Nereids we met in chapter I. Tritons often accompanied the great deities when they traveled over the sea. The Roman writer Apuleius described a watery procession of Tritons surrounding Venus, the goddess of love: "Bands of [Tritons] sported here and there on the waters, one softly blowing on his echoing shell, another fending off with silk parasol the heat of the hostile sun, a third holding a

mirror before his mistress's face, while others, yoked in pairs to her chariot, swam below."

Monsters and Storm Bringers

There were mythical, divine Tritons, and then there was the Triton of Tanagra, a tourist attraction in second-century Greece. Pickled and preserved, it had supposedly attacked ships and swimmers before it was killed. A Greek writer named Pausanias saw not only this pickled Triton but another one "among the curiosities at Rome." Such creatures were not the handsome mermen that frolicked with Nereids and goddesses. Instead, said Pausanias, "On their heads they grow hair like that of marsh frogs. . . . The rest of their body is rough with fine scales just as is the shark. Under their ears they have gills and a man's nose; but the mouth is broader and the teeth are those of a beast. . . . Under the breast and belly is a tail like a dolphin's instead of feet."

This grinning, grotesque Triton appears in a fourteenth-century Dutch manuscript.

The mermen of later centuries tended to be equally grotesque and were often described as monsters. A thirteenth-century manuscript from Iceland had this to say about the merman: "The monster is tall and of great size and rises straight out of the water. . . . It has shoulders like a man's but no hands. Its body apparently grows narrower from the shoulders down, so that the lower down it has been observed, the more slender it has seemed to be. . . . Whenever the monster has shown itself, men have always been sure that a storm would follow."

Bishop Erik Pontoppidan labeled many reports of mermen "idle tales," but he also believed there had been sightings by reliable eyewitnesses. He noted, for example, the testimony that three Danish boatmen made to a town official in 1723. They swore they had seen a merman "like an old man, with short curled hair . . . with a black beard that looked as if it had been trimmed." When the merman dove under the water, they saw his pointed fish tail.

Mermen were believed to inhabit the New World as well as the Old. In 1782 a French-Canadian trapper named Venant St. Germain saw one in Lake Superior. He described that merman in a sworn statement before two judges, who wrote:

> It had half its body out of the water, and the novelty of so extraordinary a spectacle excited [St. Germain's] attention and led him to examine it carefully. The body of the animal seemed to him to be about the size of a child of seven or eight years of age. . . . The eyes were extremely brilliant; the nose small but handsomely shaped; the mouth proportional to the rest of the face; the complexion of a brownish hue, the ears well formed.

St. Germain wanted to shoot the creature, but a Native American woman among his traveling companions stopped him, saying that the little merman was the "god of the waters and lakes." The fact they had seen it, she added, meant that a deadly storm was coming, and if they stayed near the beach the waves would surely sweep them out into the lake and drown them. Luckily, their camp was at the top of a steep bank, so the fierce three-day storm that began that night did them little harm.

The Forsaken Merman

"Agnes and the Merman," a Danish ballad from the late 1700s, told the tale of a merman who married a human woman and took her to live with him under the sea. Eventually, however, she deserted him and their children. The story inspired nineteenth-century English poet Matthew Arnold to write one of his most famous works, "The Forsaken Merman." Here is an excerpt:

> Come, dear children, let us away;
> Down and away below!
> Now my brothers call from the bay,
> Now the great winds shoreward blow,
> Now the salt tides seaward flow;
> Now the wild white horses play,
> Champ and chafe and toss in the spray.
> Children dear, let us away!
> This way, this way!

Above: A 1920 illustration of "The Forsaken Merman," showing his human wife with her merbaby on her lap.

Call her once before you go—
Call once yet!
In a voice that she will know;
"Margaret! Margaret!"
Children's voices should be dear
(Call once more) to a mother's ear;
Children's voices, wild with pain—
Surely she will come again!
Call her once and come away;
This way, this way!
"Mother dear, we cannot stay!

Come, dear children, come away down;
Call no more!
One last look at the white-walled town,
And the little gray church on the windy shore;
Then come down!
She will not come though you call all day;
Come away, come away! . . .

Come away, away children;
Come children, come down!
The hoarse wind blows coldly;
Lights shine in the town.
She will start from her slumber
When gusts shake the door;
She will hear the winds howling,
Will hear the waves roar.
We shall see, while above us
The waves roar and whirl,
A ceiling of amber,
A pavement of pearl.
Singing: "Here came a mortal,
But faithless was she!
And alone dwell for ever
The kings of the sea."

SHAPE-SHIFTERS

She lifted up her head and stretched her arms to the sea,
She was changed to a seal as I watched from afar:
Dividing the waves, O strongly went she
To the boundless spaces where her kindred are.
~"Lament of the Sealwoman's Lover,"
folk song from the Isle of Man

MERPEOPLE COULD SOMETIMES CHANGE their forms from part fish to fully human, as Melusine had done. A type of Irish merperson called a merrow was also able to take a different shape when it came onto land—but it was not a human shape. According to the Irish poet William Butler Yeats, merrows were at one time well known "on the wilder coasts of Ireland."

The male Merrows . . . have green teeth, green hair, pig's eyes, and red noses; but their women are beautiful, for all their fish tails and little duck-like scales between their fingers. . . . Sometimes they come out of the sea, and wander about the

Opposite:
Austrian artist
Gustav Klimt's 1899
painting of water
spirits conveys the
unsettling beauty
of such creatures.

shore in the shape of little hornless cows. They have, when in their own shape, a red cap . . . usually covered with feathers. If this is stolen, they cannot again go down under the waves.

Shape-shifting was an ability common to other types of sea people who were closely related to mermaids. For example, Brazilian folklore tells of *encantados*, dolphins who could turn into people and sometimes married humans. Similarly, there was a Hawaiian legend about a shark king who was able to become a handsome young man. In this form he came ashore and fell in love with a beautiful young woman. They married, and in time had a son who also possessed the ability to shape-shift between human and shark.

The Seal Folk

Perhaps the most famous shape-shifting sea people are the selkies of the British Isles. Selkies were normally seals, but they were capable of coming onto land and taking human form. In some places it was believed there were only certain times when selkies could do this, such as full-moon nights. One of the selkies' favorite land activities was to sing and dance the night away. In many stories, female selkies—who were famously beautiful—would take on human form during the daytime, when they liked to leave the salty sea and wash in fresh stream water.

To become human, selkies had to shed their sealskins, which they carefully hid. Anyone finding such a skin had power over the selkie, who was unable to return to the sea without it. A folklorist who gathered songs and stories from the Hebrides Islands of Scotland explained in a 1909 book, "The Islesman in whom goodness is stronger than love, finding the sealwoman bathing in the creek, will let her go back to her own natural element; the Islesman in whom love is stronger than goodness cunningly hides her skin, and weds her on the third night after he has found her."

Many people in Scotland, Ireland, and elsewhere were thought to be descended from the children of such marriages. But no matter how much a selkie wife loved her family, she always longed for the sea. If she could find her skin, she would immediately put it on and plunge back into the waves forever. Yet, in seal form, she might still visit and help her husband and children. In one story, a selkie who is about to return to the sea tells her little son that whenever he and his father do not have enough food, they should set out their net by a certain rock, "and thy mother will throw into it the choice fish that will make a laddie grow, and a man pleased with himself."

The waves themselves seem to form this maiden of the sea.

Male selkies seem to have had an easier time avoiding being trapped on land. They tended to come and go as they pleased, especially to marry human women. Although a selkie rarely stayed with his mortal wife, he might return to her from time to time. Often the wife did not even know that her husband was one of the seal people, as in "The Grey Selkie of Skule Skerrie." In this old Scottish ballad, a young woman sings a lullaby to her baby, then goes to bed, wondering where the child's father is. That night the selkie enters her room:

Sayin' "Awake, awake, my pretty maid,
For oh, how sound as thou dost sleep!
An' I'll tell thee where thy baby's father is—
He's sittin' close at thy bed feet!"

When the woman asks her husband where he lives, he tells her he earns his living out of the sea, and then confesses, "I am a man upon the land, I am a selkie in the sea."

The Water Horse

In Scotland there were tales not only of selkies but also of the *each uisge*, or water horse. With a fish's tail but a horse's head, chest, and hind legs, this creature lived in the sea, sea inlets, and the deep Scottish lakes. A similar creature, the kelpie, lived in rivers and streams. Like many merpeople, these beasts could both warn of storms and cause them. They were also known to make rivers and lakes overflow, in order to sweep people away in the floods.

The *each uisge* and kelpie were not very friendly to humans. They would appear on land looking like normal horses—but the handsomest horses imaginable, decked out with fine saddles and bridles. This was all a trick to lure unsuspecting people onto their backs. If the creature was successful, its passenger was in for a terrifying high-speed ride

A kelpie, as imagined by an American illustrator around 1880.

that would end with the horse's plunging into the water to drown and then eat the rider.

Once mounted on the beast's back, there was almost no hope of getting off again. Some stories said you could break a kelpie's power by saying its true name out loud. If you didn't know that name, however, you might have to follow the example of the man who escaped a water horse by cutting off his own fingers, which remained gripping the bridle as he fell safely to the ground.

One of the most terrifying things about the water horse was that it could also take the form of a handsome young man. In this way it would tempt women to the waterside, and then drag them into the depths. So if a girl were to meet an attractive stranger, she was wise to check to make sure that he was really human. If he had seaweed in his hair or smelled like saltwater, he was probably a water horse in disguise.

Various kinds of water horses—nearly all of which behaved like the Scottish ones—appeared in the folklore of Scandinavia, Wales, Ireland, and even the eastern United States. Belief in these creatures was not only widespread but survived a very long time. A scholar studying an Irish community in the 1960s reported that people there said, "Until 40 years ago [the water horse] lived in the fresh water lake . . . where it was seen on certain nights traveling abreast the surface with its head held high and mane waving in the wind. Now it is seen only at sea and infrequently at great distance."

A WATERY WORLD

We have lingered in the chambers of the sea
By sea-girls wreathed with seaweed red and brown.
~T. S. Eliot, "The Love Song of J. Alfred Prufrock," 1917

IN THE NINETEENTH CENTURY, MANY PEOPLE still believed that merfolk and their kin existed as actual living creatures. In some places this belief lasted even into the twentieth century. Most people, though, came to regard mermaids as beings of myth and legend. Yet as fantastic creatures, mermaids have continued to fascinate us—perhaps more than ever. They have inspired artists, poets, novelists, filmmakers, and even advertisers. Mermaid stories are still told and retold, and mermaid lore has been collected from around the world. So if you love mermaids, don't worry: there will always be more for you to find out about them.

Opposite:
To some people, the mermaid's mirror was a symbol of vanity, but originally it may have represented the moon, the planet Venus, or enlightened knowledge of the self.

MERMAIDS OF MANY CULTURES

Since roughly three-quarters of our planet is covered in water, it is no surprise that people in almost every part of the world have myths, legends, and folklore about water spirits of some kind or other. We have met a number of them in this book already, and now we'll meet a few more.

The Book of the Marvels of India, written in Arabic about a thousand years ago, tells how a trading ship was blown off course and landed on a mysterious island. There the sailors beheld "the most beautiful slaves we had ever seen, and the merriest. . . . Only their heads were tiny, and below their flanks, they had a kind of wing or fluke like turtles." In spite of this oddity, the captain purchased the slaves. As soon as the ship was back out at sea, though, the captives all jumped overboard. The sailors heard them singing, clapping, and laughing in the water. Then a storm came up, blowing the ship on its way and leaving the women to enjoy their freedom.

In *A Voyage to the Congo,* published in 1682, Italian priest Jerome Merolla described his efforts to convert the people of central Africa to Christianity. Among his experiences was a visit to a kingdom that was "altogether governed by the female sex." This kingdom, Merolla added, was home to the source of the Zaire River, throughout which "there is to be found the mermaid."

Mermaids were also known in other parts of Africa. The Zulus of southern Africa believed mermaids granted healing powers to certain people. In Nigeria there was a goddess named Igbaghon whose kingdom beneath the river was the underworld; mermaids served her and kept watch over her realm. Other parts of West Africa had tales of a number of merpeople and water spirits, including a mermaid goddess named Mami Wata, or Mother Water.

In China, water spirits were generally imagined as dragons. This was largely true in Japan, too. There was, however, a Japanese mermaidlike being called the Ningyo, pictured as a large fish with a woman's head. Said to be very beautiful, she was also thought of as a kindly being who protected humans and warned them of dangers both on sea and land.

Equally benevolent were the Halfway People in the traditions of eastern Canada's Micmac Indians. Human from the waist up, fish from the waist down, the Halfway People looked after fisherfolk, singing to alert them whenever a storm was coming. Only if the Halfway People were treated badly would they cause harm to humans.

Another kind of spirit needed no excuse at all to harm people. Usually called the nixie, from the German form of its name, it appears in legends from Germany, Switzerland, and Scandinavia. Nixies could be fish-tailed or human-legged. They were able to tell the future and, like mermaids, spent a great deal of time combing their hair and singing. Their loveliness, however, was a mirage, disguising their shriveled appearance and green skin, teeth, and hair. They usually lived in lakes, and their main purpose in life was to lure people into the water and drown them.

Similar to the nixie was a Russian spirit called the *rusalka*. A famous 1819 poem by the Russian writer Alexander Pushkin told how a beautiful rusalka tempted and tormented an elderly monk. He had settled in an isolated grove beside a lake, intending to spend the rest of his life alone in prayer. But the rusalka emerged from the water, smiling, waving, beckoning, and calling to him. Soon he could think of nothing except "the wondrous girl." Here is how the story ends:

On the third day the ardent hermit
Was sitting on the shore, in love,
Awaiting the voluptuous mermaid,
As shade was lying on the grove.
Night ceded to the sun's emergence;
By then the monk had disappeared.
It's said a crowd of local urchins
Saw floating there a wet grey beard.

A Lasting Song

Let's return now to Greece, the home of some of the earliest tales about maidens of the sea. Beginning in ancient times, the young conqueror Alexander the Great was a heroic figure, and his adventures became more and more fantastic over the centuries. Even in the modern era, the people of Greece have continued to tell stories about him, many based on legends hundreds of years old. This folktale is one of them.

Alexander had gone on a quest to obtain a jarful of the water of immortality. Exhausted when he got home, he left the jar sitting on a table. While he was sleeping, his sister found the water. Not knowing what it was, she drank some of it and used the rest to wash her long, beautiful hair. When Alexander woke up and went to drink the water, he was furious to find out what his sister had done. "May half your body turn into a fish and as long as this world exists, may you wander the seas without rest," he shouted.

Instantly the girl turned into a mermaid. Despite her transformation, she continued to love her brother, and ever since then she has stopped ships to ask the crew if Alexander is still alive. If the sailors answer that he is dead, she creates a storm to sink their vessel. But if they give her the answer she wants, telling her that her brother continues to thrive, she "stops the wind, smoothes the waves, and accompanies the ship, singing and playing her harp. And whenever someone sings a new song, people often say that he must have heard it from Alexander's sister, the mermaid."

This story has nearly everything we've come to expect from mermaid lore: her beautiful hair, her temper, her ability both to cause storms and to calm the sea, and, above all, her marvelous music. Anyone who has spent time beside the ocean or a burbling stream or a rushing river knows how amazing the sound of water can be. No wonder the greatest power of the mermaid, spirit of the wild waters, is the magic of music.

The Little Mermaid

No book about mermaids would be complete without mentioning Hans Christian Andersen's 1835 fairy tale "The Little Sea Maid," which was the inspiration for Disney's 1989 movie *The Little Mermaid*. In Andersen's original story, the sea maid was a daughter of the Sea King and lived in a splendid palace at the bottom of the ocean. On her fifteenth birthday she swam to the surface of the water, where she saw a handsome young prince on board a ship. The sea maid watched him for hours, until a ferocious storm came up and dashed the ship to pieces. As it sank, the sea maid pulled the prince out of the wreckage and got him safely to shore.

After that the sea maid thought constantly about the prince and the human world. One day she asked her grandmother if humans died the same way sea people did. The old sea woman said yes, with one great difference: "We have not an immortal soul; we never

receive another life. . . . Men, on the contrary, have a soul which lives for ever."

Now the sea maid yearned for an immortal soul even more than she longed to see the prince again. Her grandmother explained that the only way she could get her heart's desire was if a human man loved and married her—then he would share his soul with her, and she would be able to share in humanity's eternal happiness. "But that can never come to pass. What is considered beautiful here in the sea—the fish-tail—they would consider ugly on the earth: they don't understand it."

The sea maid went for help to the sea witch, who agreed to make a brew to transform her tail into legs but warned that, although the sea maid would be supremely graceful, every step would be as painful as if knives were cutting her feet. Also, if she failed to win the prince's love and he married someone else, on the very next morning she would turn into sea foam. Finally, the sea maid must pay for the brew by giving her voice to the sea witch.

The sea maid accepted these conditions. She swam to the beach below the prince's castle and there drank the brew, which made her faint. When she awoke, she was fully human, and the prince was standing beside her. She could answer none of the questions he asked her, for she was now mute. Nevertheless the prince took her to his castle. That evening the sea maid danced for him and his court, and although each step caused her intense pain, she was more graceful than any dancer the people had ever seen. The prince was enchanted, and the sea maid became his constant companion.

Although the prince was extremely fond of the sea maid, he thought of her as just a lovable child. He was already in love with someone else, anyway: a girl he'd seen when he awoke after his

shipwreck—the girl he thought had saved his life. With no voice, the sea maid had no way to tell him the truth. Besides, she wanted him to be happy. So when he set sail to the girl's country to marry her, the sea maid accompanied him. The bride came aboard his ship, and there the wedding was held. The sea maid danced at the celebration, even though she knew "it was the last evening she should breathe the same air with him, and behold the starry sky and the deep sea; and everlasting night without thought or dream awaited her, for she had no soul, and could win none."

The sea witch tells the little sea maid the price she must pay to try to win her prince and her soul.

After everyone went to bed, she was standing by the ship's rail when her sisters rose to the water's surface. They had all cut their hair and given it to the sea witch in return for a magic knife that would allow the sea maid to regain her tail and return home. All she had to do was thrust the knife into the prince's heart before sunrise. She was tempted, and almost did it. Then she threw the knife away into the waves, and a moment later jumped into the water herself.

The sun was coming up. Her body dissolved into foam. But something unexpected happened. She felt herself rising into the warm air, and there were hundreds of glorious beings floating over and around her. They told her they were the daughters of the air. Like the sea people, they had no immortal souls—but they had the ability to change this by doing good deeds. Now, thanks to her endurance and self-sacrifice, the sea maid was one of them. For three hundred years she would be a spirit doing good for humanity, and then at last she would gain a soul and reach paradise.

Glossary

ballad A song that tells a story.

epic A long poem about the adventures of one or more legendary heroes.

folklorist Someone who studies traditional stories, songs, beliefs, and practices.

lagoon A sheltered and relatively shallow inlet of the sea.

lyre A small, harplike musical instrument.

manuscript A handwritten book.

myth A sacred story; a story about divine or semidivine beings.

mythology A body or collection of myths, such as the myths of a particular people.

naturalist Someone who studies plants, animals, or other aspects of nature.

Scandinavia The northern European countries of Sweden, Denmark, Norway, Finland, and Iceland.

scriptures Religious writings; holy books.

Trojan War A legendary ancient war in which Greek forces battled the city of Troy (in what is now western Turkey) for ten years.

To Learn More about Mermaids

Books

Knudsen, Shannon. *Mermaids and Mermen.* Minneapolis: Lerner, 2010.

Miller, Karen. *Monsters and Water Beasts: Creatures of Fact or Fiction?* New York: Henry Holt, 2007.

Redmond, Shirley Raye. *Mermaids.* Detroit: Kidhaven Press, 2008.

Websites

American Museum of Natural History. *Mythic Creatures.*
www.amnh.org/exhibitions/past-exhibitions/mythic-creatures

Ashliman, D. L. *Water Spirit Legends.*
www.pitt.edu/~dash/water.html

Atsma, Aaron. *Theoi Greek Mythology: Fantastic Creatures.*
www.theoi.com/greek-mythology/fantastic-creatures.html

Changeri, Heather. *The Enchanted Waters.*
www.whiterosesgarden.com/Enchanted_Waters/EW_content_pgs/
EW_INDEX_PG.htm

Shee-Eire. *The Merrow-Folk.*
www.shee-eire.com/Magic&Mythology/Fairylore/The-Merrow-Folk/
page%201.htm

Selected Bibliography

Allan, Tony. *The Mythic Bestiary: The Illustrated Guide to the World's Most Fantastical Creatures*. London: Duncan Baird, 2008.

Beck, Horace. *Folklore and the Sea*. Edison, NJ: Castle Books, 1999.

Benwell, Gwen, and Arthur Waugh. *Sea Enchantress: The Tale of the Mermaid and Her Kin*. New York: Citadel Press, 1965.

Cherry, John, ed. *Mythical Beasts*. San Francisco: Pomegranate Artbooks, 1995.

Colburn, Kerry. *Mermaids: Sirens of the Sea*. Philadelphia: Courage Books, 2003.

Dobell, Steve. *Mermaids: An Anthology of Verse and Prose*. London: Southwater, 2004.

Ellis, Richard. *Monsters of the Sea*. New York: Alfred A. Knopf, 1994.

Meurger, Michel, and Claude Gagnon. *Lake Monster Traditions: A Cross-Cultural Analysis*. London: Fortean Tomes, 1988.

Nigg, Joseph. *The Book of Dragons and Other Mythical Beasts*. Hauppauge, NY: Barron's, 2002.

—-. *The Book of Fabulous Beasts: A Treasury of Writings from Ancient Times to the Present*. New York: Oxford University Press, 1999.

Ratisseau, Elizabeth. *Mermaids*. Seattle: Laughing Elephant Books, 2003.

Rose, Carol. *Giants, Monsters, and Dragons: An Encyclopedia of Folklore, Legend, and Myth*. New York: W. W. Norton, 2000.

South, Malcolm, ed. *Mythical and Fabulous Creatures: A Sourcebook and Research Guide*. New York: Peter Bedrick Books, 1988.

Thomson, David. *The People of the Sea: A Journey in Search of the Seal Legend*. Washington, DC: Counterpoint, 2000.

Varner, Gary R. *Creatures in the Mist: Little People, Wild Men and Spirit Beings around the World: A Study in Comparative Mythology*. New York: Algora Publishing, 2007.

Notes on Quotations

For ease of reading, spelling, punctuation, and capitalization have been modernized in many of the quotations from older sources.

Chapter 1

p. 9 "[I] heard a mermaid": *A Midsummer Night's Dream*, act 2, scene 1, in William Shakespeare, *The Complete Works: Compact Edition*, edited by Stanley Wells and others (Oxford: Clarendon Press, 1988).

p. 9 "combing out their hair": J. M. Barrie, *Peter Pan*, chap. 8, www.gutenberg.org/files/16/16-h.htm#2HCH0008

p. 10 "in a curious form": Benwell, *Sea Enchantress*, p. 28.

p. 10 "and it is for this reason": Ibid., p. 29.

p. 12 "a fiction; only in them": Pliny the Elder, *The Natural History* 9.4, translated by John Bostock, www.perseus.tufts.edu

p. 12 "a considerable number": Ibid.

p. 12 "moving in the water": Benwell, *Sea Enchantress*, p. 31.

p. 12 "Where your gold": Ibid.

Chapter 2

p. 15 "Featherless birds": Cherry, *Mythical Beasts*, p. 154.

p. 16 "bird-maidens . . . [whose] music": Colburn, *Mermaids*, p. 44.

p. 16 "The siren, who sings": Ratisseau, *Mermaids*, p. 34.

p. 17 "who bewitch everybody": Benwell, *Sea Enchantress*, p. 42.

p. 17 "Come hither, come": Nigg, *The Book of Fabulous Beasts*, p. 29.

p. 17 "So spoke they": Ibid.

p. 18 "The sound of Orpheus": Colburn, *Mermaids*, p. 48.

p. 18 "We know all things": Allan, *The Mythic Bestiary*, p. 224.

p. 19 "It was not the sweetness": Cherry, *Mythical Beasts*, p. 148.

p. 19 "Come to the land": Dobell, *Mermaids*, p. 40.

p. 19 "longed not to take": Colburn, *Mermaids*, p. 44.

p. 21 "High yonder in wondrous seeming": Dobell, *Mermaids*, p. 44.

Chapter 3

p. 23 "Then up . . . raised": Helen Child Sargent and George Lyman Kittredge, *English and Scottish Popular Ballads Edited from the Collection of Francis James Child* (Boston: Houghton Mifflin, 1904), p. 648.

p. 25 "wherever she went": Benwell, *Sea Enchantress*, p. 61.

p. 25 "expecting every moment": Ibid., p. 63.

p. 25 "bodily ease," "fat horses," : Ibid., p. 70.

p. 26 "So great is our delight": Ibid., p. 70.

p. 26 "This wonderful beast": Nigg, *The Book of Fabulous Beasts*, p. 141.

p. 27 "first they cleansed," "she would obey," and "would often strive": Benwell, *Sea Enchantress*, p. 81.

p. 29 "sitting on the unruffled surface": John Rhys, *Celtic Folklore: Welsh and Manx*, vol. I (Oxford: Clarendon Press, 1901), p. 3.

p. 29 "because people" and "that he touched her": Ibid., p. 10.

Chapter 4

p. 31 "The mermaids and men-fish": Benwell, *Sea Enchantress*, p. 97.

p. 32 "from the navel upward": South, *Mythical and Fabulous Creatures*, p. 137.

p. 32 "It seemed so beautiful": Nigg, *The Book of Fabulous Beasts*, pp. 259–260.

p. 33 "This (I suppose)" and "I know not": Ibid., p. 260.

p. 33 "swimming with all possible" and "from below the waist": Benwell, *Sea Enchantress*, p. 97.

p. 33 "Some have supposed": Ibid.

p. 34 "by the thickening": Ibid., p. 98.

p. 34 "to work strange feats": Ibid., p. 99.

p. 34 "It lived on land": Ellis, *Monsters of the Sea*, p. 80.

p. 34 "There are several hundreds": Meurger and Gagnon, *Lake Monster Traditions*, p. 18.

p. 34 "fable and fantasy": Lisbet Koerner, *Linnaeus: Nature and Nation* (Cambridge, MA: Harvard University Press, 1999), p. 93.

p. 35 "I saw three sirens": Ellis, *Monsters of the Sea*, p. 88.

p. 35 "The hands seem": Benwell, *Sea Enchantress*, p. 74.

Chapter 5

p. 37 "Amongst sea-monsters which are": Ellis, *Monsters of the Sea*, p. 80.

p. 38 "This Being in the daytime": Benwell, *Sea Enchantress*, p. 24.

p. 39 "his shoulders barnacled": Ovid, *Metamorphoses* 1.332–341, quoted at www.theoi.com/Pontios/Triton.html

p. 39 "Bands of [Tritons] sported": Apuleius, *The Golden Ass* 4.31 ff., quoted at www.theoi.com/Pontios/Tritones.html

p. 40 "among the curiosities " and "On their heads": Pausanias, *Description of Greece* 9.20, quoted at www.theoi.com/Thaumasios/Tritones.html

p. 40 "The monster is tall": Ellis, *Monsters of the Sea*, 77.

p. 41 "idle tales": Ibid., p. 80.

p. 41 "like an old man": Meurger and Gagnon, *Lake Monster Traditions*, p. 19.

p. 41 "It had half its body": Frederick Stonehouse, *Haunted Lakes: Great Lakes Ghost Stories, Superstitions and Sea Serpents* (Duluth, MN: Lake Superior Port Cities, 1997), p. 169.

p. 41 "god of the waters": Ibid.

p. 42 "Come, dear children": Alexander Allison and others, eds., *The Norton Anthology of Poetry*, rev. ed. (New York: W. W. Norton, 1975), pp. 836–839.

Chapter 6

p. 45 "She lifted up her head": Benwell, *Sea Enchantress*, p. 22.

p. 45 "on the wilder coasts" and "The male Merrows": Colburn, *Mermaids*, p. 55.

p. 46 "The Islesman in whom": Thomson, *The People of the Sea*, p. 208.

p. 47 "and thy mother will throw": Ibid.

p. 48 "Sayin' 'Awake, awake'" and "I am a man": Ibid., p. 200.

p. 49 "Until 40 years ago": Varner, *Creatures in the Mist*, p. 23.

Chapter 7

p. 51 "We have lingered": T. S. Eliot, *The Wasteland and Other Poems* (New York: Harcourt Brace Jovanovich, 1962), p. 9.

p. 52 "the most beautiful slaves": Benwell, *Sea Enchantress*, pp. 66–67.

p. 52 "altogether governed" and "there is to be found": Ibid., p. 101.

p. 53 "the wondrous girl": Alexander Pushkin, "Rusalka," translated by Genia Gurarie, http://clover.slavic.pitt.edu/tales/rusalka.html

p. 54 "On the third day": Ibid.

p. 54 "May half your body": *Folktales from Greece: A Treasury of Delights*, retold by Soula Mitakidou and others (Greenwood Village, CO: Libraries Unlimited, 2002), p. 95.

p. 55 "stops the wind": Ibid.

p. 55 "We have not an immortal": Hans Christian Andersen, *The Complete Illustrated Works* (London: Chancellor Press, 1994), p. 550.

p. 56 "But that can never": Ibid., p. 551.

p. 57 "it was the last evening": Ibid., p. 558.

Index

ABOUT THE AUTHOR

KATHRYN HINDS grew up near Rochester, New York. She studied music and writing at Barnard College, and went on to do graduate work in comparative literature and medieval studies at the City University of New York. She has written more than forty books for young people, including *Everyday Life in the Roman Empire*, *Everyday Life in the Renaissance*, *Everyday Life in Medieval Europe*, and the books in the series BARBARIANS, LIFE IN THE MEDIEVAL MUSLIM WORLD, LIFE IN ELIZABETHAN ENGLAND, and LIFE IN ANCIENT EGYPT. Kathryn lives in the north Georgia mountains with her husband, their son, and two cats. When she is not reading or writing, she enjoys dancing, gardening, knitting, and taking walks in the woods. Visit Kathryn online at www.kathrynhinds.com

FOX GRADIN, CELESTIAL STUDIOS PHOTOGRAPHY